# Jest for the Pun of It

## Wordplay for Those Who Dare

by
Meridith Montague

This book is dedicated to my parents, Joyce and George Montague who first instilled in me the love of the English language and the need to use a dictionary.

# Table of Contents

# Introduction

A pun is simply a play on words. This form of humor takes advantage of the fact that words and phrases can, at times, sound alike but have very different meanings.

With its extensive use of idioms, clichés, synonyms, homonyms and words adopted from other languages around the globe, English is perfect for a punster.

From prime ministers to presidents, from humorists to literary giants like Shakespeare and Oscar Wilde, those who speak and write in the English tongue have, throughout history, enjoyed engaging in a bit of word play.

To those who disparage this form of humor, I can only quote the multi-talented musician and humorist, Oscar Levant who said, "A pun is the lowest form of humor – when you didn't think of it first." Or there's Alfred Hitchcock's opinion of this type of humor, "Puns are the highest form of literature."

But I like poet and journalist, Christopher Morley's definition, "A pun is language on vacation."

Knowing you will always be in good company, Go ye forth and pun proudly!!

# Riddles and Dad Jokes

"Dad jokes" are fun and predictable jokes, usually based on puns that can be understood by the younger set. These, sometimes presented in the form of simple riddles, are some of the first jokes learned by children. They give kids their first chance to appreciate language and humor.

When does a joke become a 'dad joke'?
*When it becomes apparent.*

What building has the most stories?
*The library.*

What dinosaur knows the most synonyms?
*The thesaurus.*

What was the puppy's favorite movie?
*Hairy Paw-ter and the Philosopher's Bone by J.K. Growling*

What did the Dalmatian say to the masseuse?
*That's the spot.*

. ° ⚠ ° .

When do you see the dentist about your dog?
*When the canine gets loose.*

. ° ⚠ ° .

It's raining cats and dogs.
Watch out you don't step in a poodle.

. ° ⚠ ° .

What is it called when a huge number of dad jokes
goes viral?
*A pun-demic.*

. ° ⚠ ° .

I used to tell jokes about broken clocks.
But none of them worked.

. ° ⚠ ° .

My dog's a magician.
I call him a labracadabrador.

Tempers rose and the dog's picnic quickly turned into a Bark-B-Q.

.° ⚛ °.

I put a name tag on my dog; now she has collar ID.

.° ⚛ °.

Animal jokes have a lot of pet-tential.

.° ⚛ °.

Why do Dachshund's like the shade?
*They're hot dogs.*

.° ⚛ °.

It was movie night and the dogs were excited.
We were going to take them to see Jurassic Bark.

.° ⚛ °.

Did you just buy your dog a new car?
*No, we leashed it.*

.° ⚛ °.

What rank did the pirate dog have?
*He was fur-st mate.*

Why did the dog climb a ladder?
*He was a roofer.*

Why do dogs pee on trees?
*They like the bark.*

What did the dog get when he graduated college?
*A pedigree.*

What do you call a drone that can't make up its mind?
*A may-bee.*

The dog always felt patriotic when he heard the Star Spaniel-ed Banner.

What kind of photographers do young dogs dislike?
*The puppy-razzi.*

The dog who ran to get her new outfit. Was fetching.

Why did the dog go to the bank?
*To make a de-paw-sit.*

What did the Collie say to the Basset?
*Stop hounding me.*

Why was the puppy so tired?
*He had a ruff day.*

Where did they take the puppy who hurt his paw?
*To the dog-tor.*

Why was the Dalmatian so bad at hide a seek?
*He was always spotted.*

What wild cat can never be trusted?
*The cheetah.*

. ° ❀ ° .

What's a vampire's favorite dog?
*The bloodhound.*

. ° ❀ ° .

What's a spy's favorite dog?
*The Pekingese.*

. ° ❀ ° .

What animal got a job working in the boatyard?
*The docks-hund.*

. ° ❀ ° .

What do canines say to each other at Christmas.
*"Feliz Navidog."*

. ° ❀ ° .

Where do dogs go for a cup of coffee?
*Star-Barks.*

. ° ❀ ° .

What was the puppy's favorite movie?
*The Hound of Music.*

. ° ☣ ° .

What did the waiter say to the family at the dog's birthday party?
*Bone Appe'tit!*

. ° ☣ ° .

Who is the world's greatest detective?
*Sherlock Bones.*

. ° ☣ ° .

Why did the dog go to the modern art museum?
*He wanted to see the paintings of Andy Warhowl.*

. ° ☣ ° .

Why do dogs prefer giving birth indoors?
*They don't want to be ticketed for littering.*

. ° ☣ ° .

Where do dogs keep their cars?
*Grr-ages or barking lots.*

. ° ☣ ° .

Why did the music-lover keep dogs and birds?
*He needed the woofers and tweeters.*

. ° ❀ ° .

What dog is most likely to become a cheerleader?
*The Pom-Pomeranian.*

. ° ❀ ° .

Why didn't the dog bark?
*She was a Malamute.*

. ° ❀ ° .

Why was the dog so anxious to move to Copenhagen?
*He was a Great Dane.*

. ° ❀ ° .

How is a pig's tail like getting up before dawn?
*It's twirly.*

. ° ❀ ° .

What did the parrot say after losing a boxing match
with a dog?
*I fought the paw and the paw won.*

What kind of dog likes to fight?
*The Boxer.*

Which states are favorite among dogs?
*Collie-fornia and Barkansas.*

What type of car did the rich dog buy?
*A Furr-rari.*

What did the young dogs snack on during the movie?
*Pup-corn.*

I knew I told a good joke, when my Collie barked with laughter.

That story about your dog retrieving a stick from a mile away is a little far-fetched.

Why did the Dachshund win all his races.
*He was a real wiener.*

What animal makes noise when it breathes?
*The wheeze-l.*

Why was the man's living room so noisy?
*He lived in an a-bark-ment.*

Do you know what a Sheepdog does for a living?
*I herd.*

How certain is the dog that he can identify the thief?
*He's pawsitve.*

Did you see the sale at the dog show?
*Buy one; get one flea.*

What did the dog say when he picked out a new toy?
*I chews you.*

Did you hear about the two kangaroos who got married?
*They lived hoppily ever after.*

Where does King Arthur park his dromedary?
*In a Camel-lot.*

I thought you said that was a baby goat.
*I was just kidding.*

What do you call an alligator in a vest?
*An investigator.*

Broken pencils are pointless.

I'm friends with 25 letters of the alphabet. I don't know why.

I just went to the library and my weekend is fully booked.

That stick of gum is in mint condition.

Why was the calendar nervous?
*His days were numbered.*

Why was the alarm clock nervous?
*His time was about up.*

Why is today always a gift?
*Because it's the present.*

What's the most adventurous city in Colorado?
*Boulder.*

Why didn't the student go to the football game on Halloween?
*He was afraid of the team spirit.*

When the scientist crossed poison ivy with a four-leaf clover, he had a rash of good luck.

How do you throw a space party?
*You planet.*

Why was the scarecrow never unemployed?
*He was outstanding in his field.*

What do you get when you cross a snowman and a vampire?
*Frostbite.*

.° ⚛ °.

What is the difference between unlawful and illegal?
*One is against the law, the other is a sick bird.*

What music do they listen to on the eighth planet from the sun?
*Nep-tunes.*

.° ⚛ °.

What do you get when you divide the circumference of a pumpkin with its diameter?
*Pumpkin pie.*

.° ⚛ °.

Why couldn't the bicycle stand on its own?
*It was two-tired.*

.° ⚛ °.

Why did the chicken cross the playground?
*To get to the other slide.*

.° ⚛ °.

What did the blanket say to the sheet?
*I've got you covered.*

15

What happened to the survivors of the collision between a blue ship and a red ship?
*There were marooned.*

How do attorney's dress for court?
*In a lawsuit.*

Why was the burglar walking around the outside of the house?
*He was looking for a window of opportunity.*

What kind of dog earns merit badges?
*A Beagle Scout.*

Why can you never trust an atom?
*They make up everything.*

Why did the boy put a miniature Slinky in each shoe?
*He wanted to add a little spring to his step.*

How funny are small mountains?
*Hillarious.*

Why did the bee get married?
*He found his honey.*

How do fix a broken sousaphone?
*With a tuba-glue.*

Why didn't the builder trust stairs or elevators?
*They were always up to something.*

How does the moon cut his hair?
*Eclipse it.*

What do dogs do when they need a break while watching a movie?
*They put it on paws.*

Knock, knock.
Who's there?
Banana.
Banana who?
Knock, knock.
Who's there?
Banana.
Banana who?
(repeat one more time)
Knock, knock.
Who's there?
Orange?
Orange who?
Orange you glad I didn't say banana again.

Why did the clock get shushed in the library?
*It was tocking too loud.*

What did the cupcake say to the frosting?
*I'd be muffin without you!*

What does a skunk judge say?
*Odor in the court!*

What do you call a duck that loves to make jokes?
*A wise-quacker.*

Who is the most famous fish spy?
*James Pond.*

Why do pirates make such good singers?
*Because they hit the high Cs!*

Two windmills are standing in a wind farm. One asks, "What's your favorite kind of music?" The other says, "I'm a big metal fan."

# It's a Sign:
# Headlines and Signs

## Headlines

These are real headlines taken from newspapers, many collected by the word play master, Richard Lederer. The humor in these is derived from the wonderful nature of the English language and stems in the main from the odd word placement or puns.

Accident at the Glue Factory Creates Sticky Situation

Police Discover Crack in New Zealand

Tuna Biting Off Alaskan Coast

Toilet Stolen from Police Station. Police Have Nowhere to Go

Grandmother of Eight Makes Hole in One

Deaf Mute Gets New Hearing in Murder Case

Safety Experts Say School Bus Passengers Should Be Belted

Traffic Dead Rise Slowly

Drunk Gets Nine Months in Violin Case

Robber Holds Up Albert's Hosiery

New Autos to Hit 5 Million

Queen Mary Having Bottom Scraped

Prostitutes Appeal to Pope

Squad Helps Dog Bite Victim

Man Eating Piranha Mistakenly Sold as Pet Fish

Two Convicts Evade Noose: Jury Hung

Many Antiques Seen at DAR Meeting

Students Cook and Serve Grandparents

Man Held Over Giant LA Brush Fire

Florida: Illegal Aliens Cut in Half by New Law

Genetic Engineering Splits Scientists

Survivor of Siamese Twins Join Parents

# Road Signs

What do you call a transparent billboard?
*A clear sign.*

What do you call a billboard displaying a giant clock?
*A sign of the times.*

What do you call a billboard that falls on you?
*A bad sign.*

How do billboards talk?
*Through sign language.*

I drove past a billboard promoting Niagara Falls as the tallest waterfall in the world.
Turns out it was falls advertising.

A billboard advertising a roadside pie shop reads:
Pi Just 3.14 Miles Away.

I got called into my boss's office about a billboard I created. It was a good sign.

What do you call a committee made up entirely of people named William? *A Billboard.*

What do you call a hobbit that works in advertising?
*Billboard Baggins.*

# Entry Into a Wooded Area: *Warning Limbs May Fall*

# Punny Store and Restaurant Names

Life of Pie

THAI TANIC

Turning Vegan Would be a Big Missed Steak

Pita Pan (The Little Restaurant That Never Grew Up)

The Codfather (Fish and Chips)

Iron Maiden (Professional Ironing Service)

Tequila Mockingbird (Liquor Store)

Frying Nemo (Fish and Chips)

Amy's Winehouse (Liquor Store)

Florist Gump

Pho Real

Bread Zeppelin (Deli)

Sew it Seams

British Hairways (Barber Shop)

**Indiana Jeans (Denim Store)**

Jabba the Cutt (Barber)

**Jack the Clipper (Barber)**

Barber Streisand

KUNG FOOD (CHINESE RESTAURANT)

Absolutely PHObulous

*Eye Carumba (Optometry)*

Spex in the City (Also Optometry)

**MATA DOORS**

ELVIS PARSLEY (GREENGROCER)

**Hindenburger (Hamburger restaurant)**

# More Signs

Outside a cheese shop: *"Ban shredded cheese. Make America grate again."*

.° ⊛ °.

Outside clothing store: *"Our bathing suit sale is just the tops."*

.° ⊛ °.

Inside antique store: *"For sale: Antique desk suitable for lady with sturdy legs and large drawers."*

.° ⊛ °.

Sign in a produce department: *"Take lettuce from the top or heads will roll."*

.° ⊛ °.

In pet shop window: *"For Sale. Eight puppies from a German Shepherd and an Alaskan Hussy."*

.° ⊛ °.

Another wonderful pet shop sign: *"Great Dames for Sale."*

.° ⊛ °.

26

And another (gotta love those pet shops): *"Dog for sale: Eats anything and is fond of children."*

.° ☣ °.

Outside a hardware store: *"Get rid of aunts: Zapper does the job in24 hours."*

.° ☣ °.

Sign in drugstore: *"We dispense with Accuracy"*.

.° ☣ °.

Sign in front of a hot dog stand, *"What Foods These Morsels Be."*

.° ☣ °.

I visited my local zoo and saw a caged piece of toast. The sign read, "Bread in Captivity". (Someone sure had a sense of humor.)

.° ☣ °.

Word order can be important – *"Mixing bowl set designed to please a cook with round bottom for efficient beating."*

.° ☣ °.

So can spelling - Help Wanted: *"Mother's Helper -*
*Peasant Working Conditions"*

Apparel manufacturer: *"We do not tear your clothes*
*with machinery; we do it carefully, by hand."*

# Malaprops

The malaprop is a special type of pun created by the use of an incorrect word in place of one with a similar sound, either unintentionally or for comedic effect.

The word malaprop comes from a character created by Richard Sheridan in his brilliant 1775 play, *The Rivals*. In the play, the character, Mrs. Malaprop frequently uses a word that doesn't have the meaning she thinks but which sounds similar to the one she intends.

Sheridan chose the name as a humorous reference to the word malapropos meaning "inappropriate", derived from the French phrase mal a' propos meaning literally *poorly placed*.

Here are a some malaprops from Mrs. Malaprop herself:

"He is the very pineapple of politeness!" Pineapple?! She subbed in this fruit name for "pinnacle."

.° ☣ °.

"She's as headstrong as an allegory on the banks of the Nile." (As far as I know, allegories don't spend time around rivers. However, alligators do.)

———— .° ⊗ °. ————

"He can tell you the perpendiculars."

———— .° ⊗ °. ————

The fireman inhaled so much smoke, he was almost sophisticated.

———— .° ⊗ °. ————

"Illiterate him quite from your memory." (obliterate)

———— .° ⊗ °. ————

Shakespeare was quite the master of language, so it's no surprise that his works contain numerous puns and other plays on words, including malaprops.

A synonym for "malaprop" is the term Dogberryism" which comes from Shakespeare's *Much Ado About Nothing*.

In this comedy, the character "Dogberry", misuses words to humorous effect, much like Mrs. Malaprop would do 200 years later.

At one point, Dogberry says, *"Our watch, sir, have indeed comprehended two auspicious persons."* There are two malapropism examples in this line: He should have said "apprehended," not "comprehended," and "suspicious" rather than "auspicious."

Politics has always been rife with unintentional misuses of language.

Former Australian Prime Minister Tony Abbott once claimed that no one *"is the suppository of all wisdom"* (One supposes he meant repository.)

Bertie Ahern, former Prime Minister of Ireland, warned his people against *"upsetting the apple tart"* of his country's economic success. (Presumably he meant *apple cart*, but who knows?)

Richard Daley, the former mayor of Chicago, once referred to a tandem bicycle as *a tantrum bicycle* and spoke of Alcoholics Anonymous as *Alcoholics Unanimous.*

Former Texas governor, Rick Perry was famous for his utterances of malapropisms; for example, he referred to some states as "lavatories of innovation and democracy".

U.S. Congresswoman, Marjory Taylor Greene has uttered several amusing malaprops including references to a "peach tree dish" (petri dish) and the "gazpacho police".

"It will take time to restore chaos and order." (President George W. Bush)

"We cannot let terrorists and rogue nations hold this nation hostile or hold our allies hostile." (President George W. Bush)

"Republicans understand the importance of bondage between a mother and child." - Dan Quayle probably meant "bonding".

"You misunderestimated me." - George W. Bush (misunderstood, I guess)

"I am mindful not only of preserving executive powers for myself, but for my predecessors as well." (President George W. Bush)

"He was a man of great statue." - Thomas Menino, Mayor of Boston

"This is unparalyzed in the state's history." - Gib Lewis, Texas Speaker of the House (unparalleled)

# More Marvelous Malaprops

Rainy weather can be hard on the sciences (sinuses).

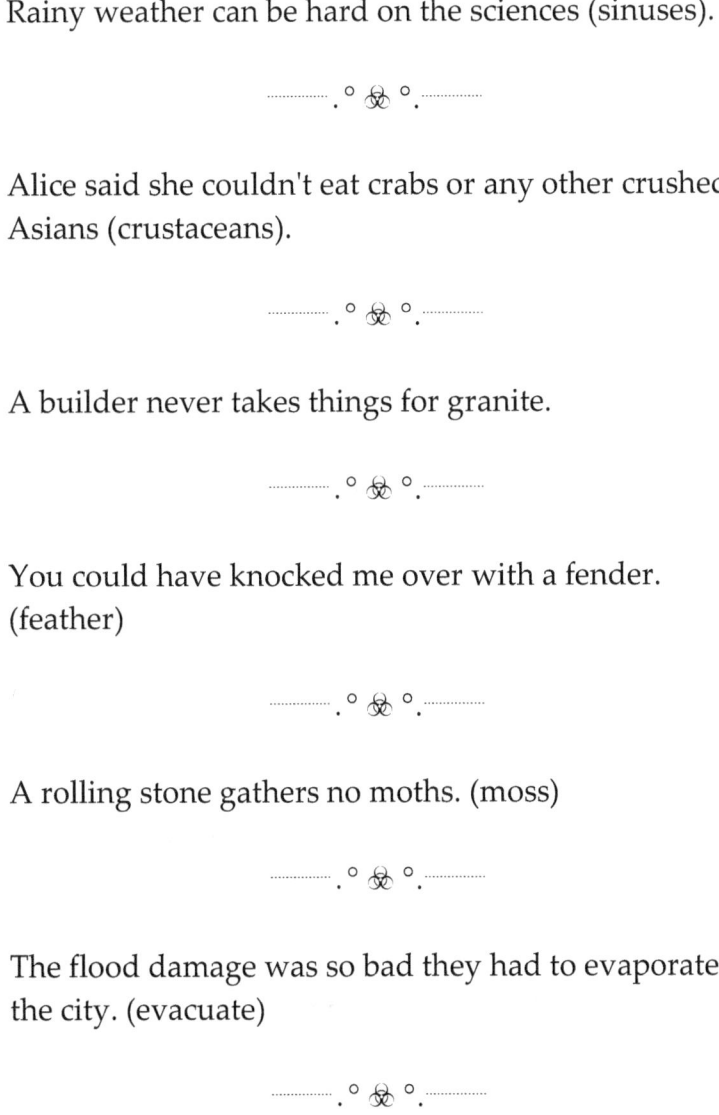

Alice said she couldn't eat crabs or any other crushed Asians (crustaceans).

A builder never takes things for granite.

You could have knocked me over with a fender. (feather)

A rolling stone gathers no moths. (moss)

The flood damage was so bad they had to evaporate the city. (evacuate)

Dad says the monster is just a pigment of my imagination. (figment)

. ° ⚠ ° .

Everybody in the company has their own cuticle. (cubicle)

. ° ⚠ ° .

I remember because I have photogenic memory. (photographic)

. ° ⚠ ° .

Flying saucers are just an optical conclusion. (illusion)

. ° ⚠ ° .

"Patience is a virgin." (virtue)

. ° ⚠ ° .

The couple took the pledge of holy acrimony.

. ° ⚠ ° .

Beware the Abdominal Snowman.

. ° ⚠ ° .

Let me see your license and resignation

.° ☣ °.

Run and get the fire distinguisher.

.° ☣ °.

If you don't like large orchestras, you have my symphony.

.° ☣ °.

I put the vegetables in the refrigerator to ruminate overnight.

.° ☣ °.

Medieval cathedrals were supported by flying buttocks.

.° ☣ °.

They had to give one of the players artificial insemination.

.° ☣ °.

He's a wealthy typhoon.

They were singing without accompaniment. You know, Acapulco.

The police surrounded the building and threw an accordion around the block.

The refugee penalized the team for unnecessary roughage.

The marriage was consummated at the altar.

In many states, murderers are put to death by electrolysis.

Growing up the lattice work were pink and yellow concubines.

The cookbook is being compiled. Please submit your favorite recipe and a short antidote concerning it.

.° ☣ °.

Apartheid is a pigment of the imagination.

.° ☣ °.

Senators are chosen as committee chairmen on the basis of senility.

.° ☣ °.

On Thanksgiving morning, you could smell foul cooking.

.° ☣ °.

Vestal virgins were pure and chased.

.° ☣ °.

Many people believe he was a satin worshiper.

.° ☣ °.

38

# Some Medical Malaprops

My health insurance plan was costing me a fortune, so I switched to HBO.

.° ☣ °.

My hospital plan will cover the cost of my last visit. It's radioactive.

.° ☣ °.

I spent so much time swimming during the summer that my crustacean tubes got infected. (Eustachian tubes)

.° ☣ °.

I was so nervous after my trip to Russia, the doctor suggested I get my heart checked with a KGB (EKG).

.° ☣ °.

My aunt got terrible heart palpitations every time she argued with her husband. They stopped after the doctor installed a peacemaker.

.° ☣ °.

The dieter ate so little he was begin to be emancipated.

.° ☣ °.

Before my grandfather died, he gave my mother his power of eternity.

.° ☣ °.

I was limping so bad, I had to get my foot x-rated.

.° ☣ °.

# Spoonerisms

Spoonerisms are words or phrases in which letters or syllables are swapped. Frequently these are done accidentally; however, this form of word play can be used effectively in humor or social commentary.

A blushing crow - a crushing blow

A farm for liars - alarm for fires

A half-warmed fish - a half-formed wish

A room with buzzers - abuzz with rumors

A deer parker - appear darker

Additional treats - traditional eats

Annual meeting - manual eating

Another deer is yawning - another year is dawning

A pair of lost wives - aware of past lives

A plate of crumbs - a crate of plumbs

Appeal in a man - a meal in a pan

Appraising mice - amazing price

Bad news for the economy! Socks stink - Bad news for
the economy! Stocks stink.

Beagle leverage - legal beverage

Bear aches - air brakes

Belly jeans - jelly beans

Bowel feast - foul beast (fowl beast)

Chalet booze - ballet shoes

Cattle ships and bruisers - battleships and cruisers

Cop porn – popcorn

Drilling a fryer - filling a dryer

Estrangement of heirs - arrangement of stairs

Eye ball - bye all

Fight in your race - right in your face

Fighting a liar - lighting a fire

Flutter by - butter fly

Go and shake a tower - go and take a shower

Hag on your bed - bag on your head

He had such mad banners - he had such bad manners

Humming and pleating - plumbing and heating

I don't want to eat parrots and keys - I don't want to eat carrots and peas.

I must mend the sail - I must send the mail

I'm a damp stealer - I'm a stamp dealer

Is the bean dizzy? - Is the dean busy?

It's kisstomary to cuss the bride – it's customary to kiss the bride

Know your blows - blow your nose

Lack of pies - pack of lies

Let me give you a hair bug - let me give you a bear hug

My zips are lipped - my lips are zipped

Nah, that's ice - Ah, that's nice

It's a nosy little cook – It's a cozy little nook

Offending attire - attending a fire

Ouch! I hit my bunny phone - Ouch! I hit my funny
bone

Our queer old dean - our dear old queen

Our shoving leopard - our loving shepherd

Please put these pants in plots - please put these
plants in pots

Raking and boasting - baking and roasting

Raging itch - aging rich

Ready! Cart your stars - Ready! Start your cars

Sighing flosser - flying saucer

Candle with hair (confusing sign on package)

Stashing clones - clashing stones

Tease my ears - ease my tears

Thank you for chewing the doors - Thank you for
doing the chores

That was a drowsy llama - that was a lousy drama

This is the pun fart - this is the fun part

This liver is wrong - this river is long

Wailing buyers - bailing wires

We must wave the sails - we must save the whales

Weather report. Expect more roaring pain. (Yikes)
Weather report. Expect more pouring rain. (Better)

Would you care for a nasal hut? - would you care for
a hazel nut?

Yak in my booth - back in my youth

You hissed my mystery lecture - you missed my
history lecture

You need to shake a tower - you need to take a
shower

You've tasted two worms - you've wasted two terms

## Yogi Berra and Samuel Goldwyn

The word play of movie mogul, Samuel Goldwyn and of Yogi Berra, the famous Yankee catcher are worthy of their own chapter.

## Yogi Berra

Lawrence Peter "Yogi" Berra was an American professional Hall of Fame baseball catcher, manager and coach. Best known to non-baseball-fans for his use (misuse) of the English language, Yogi was also prominent NY Yankee and a courageous fighter in World War II.

As a member of the military, he participated in the Normandy landings where he earned a Purple Heart.

As a baseball player, he was an 18-time All-Star and winner of 10 World Series championships.

However, his greatest fame has come down through time as the purveyor of humorous malaprops and pithy paradoxical statements.

"Take it with a *grin* of salt."

"Even Napoleon had his Watergate."

"It ain't the heat, it's the *humility*."

"Texas has a lot of *electrical* votes."

"In theory, there is no difference between theory and practice. But in practice, there is."

"I never said most of the things I said."

"Okay you guys, pair up in three."

"I'd give my right arm to be ambidextrous."

"We made too many wrong mistakes."

"I'm not going to buy my kids an encyclopedia; let them walk to school like I did."

"It's getting late early."

"He hits from both sides of the plate. He's amphibious."

"It ain't over 'til it's over."

"It's like deja vu all over again."

"A nickel ain't worth a dime anymore."

"If the fans don't want to come to the ballpark, no one can stop 'em."

"Nobody goes to that restaurant anymore; it's too crowded."

"You wouldn't have won if we'd beaten you."

"Never answer an anonymous letter."

"The future ain't what it used to be."

"It was impossible to get a conversation going, everybody was talking too much."

———— ★·☆·★ ————

# Samuel Goldwyn

Film producer, Samuel Goldwyn, also known as Samuel Goldfish, was famous for, among other things, the humorous way he often had of expressing himself. Here are some of his "Goldwynisms".

"A verbal contract is worth about as much as the paper it's written on."

"I've gone where the hand of man has never set foot."

"I'm living beyond my means, but I can afford it."

"If Roosevelt were alive today, he'd turn over in his grave."

"Coffee isn't my cup of tea."

"Color television! Bah, I won't believe it until I see it in black and white."

"If I could drop dead right now, I'd be the happiest man alive."

"Can she sing? She's practically a Florence Nightingale."

"I want to make a picture about the Russian secret police - the GOP. (Pretty sure he meant the KGB)

"The scene is dull. Tell him to put more life into his dying."

"Forecasts are difficult to make - particularly those about the future."

"Put it out of your mind. In no time, it will be a forgotten memory."

"We're overpaying him, but he's worth it."

"I've been laid up with intentional flu." (intestinal)

"Let's have some new cliche's."

"A hospital is no place to be sick."

"It's more than magnificent - it's mediocre."

"Our comedies are not to be laughed at."

"Include me out."

"Too caustic? To hell with the costs, we'll make the picture anyway."

"A bachelor's life is no life for a single man."

# Humorists, Writers and Comedians

"Refrain audacious tar your suit from pressing." - HMS Pinafore by Gilbert and Sullivan

"A pun is the lowest form of humor - unless you think of it first." - Oscar Levant

"Punning is a talent which no man affects to despise but he that is without it." — Jonathan Swift

"We must all hang together or assuredly we shall hang separately." - Ben Franklin

"Ask for me tomorrow, and you shall find me a grave man." - William Shakespeare (From Act III of Romeo and Juliet, said by Mercutio after receiving a mortal stab wound.)

"Now is the winter of our discontent/made glorious summer by this son of York" William Shakespeare punning sun and son. (Richard III)

"People in grass houses shouldn't get stoned."
— Brian Spellman

"Denial ain't just a river in Egypt." - Mark Twain

"Immanuel doesn't pun, he Kant." - Oscar Wilde

"If you are going through Hell, keep going." Winston Churchill

"Time flies like an arrow. Fruit flies like a banana." - Groucho Marx

"Hanging is too good for a man who makes puns; he should be drawn and quoted." Fred Allen

.° ⚛ °.

We had breakfast in the town of Soda, pop. 1001 - from Vladimir Nabokov's Lolita

.° ⚛ °.

"Brevity is the soul of lingerie." Dorothy Parker

.° ⚛ °.

"You can lead a horticulture but you can't make her think." Dorothy Parker

.° ⚛ °.

"Her starched petticoats giving him the slip." - Harryette Mullen "Of a Girl in White"

.° ⚛ °.

"I thought he was a young man of promise, but it appears he is a young man of promises." Arthur James Balfour

.° ⚛ °.

"The nation is prosperous on the whole, but how much prosperity is there in a hole." - Will Rogers

.° ⚠ °.

"A kleptomaniac is a person who helps himself because he can't help himself." - Henry Morgan

.° ⚠ °.

"When I am dead, I hope it may be said: "His sins were scarlet, but his books were read." - Hilaire Belloc

.° ⚠ °.

"TB or not TB, that is the question." House MD

.° ⚠ °.

Rumack: Can you fly this plane, and land it?
Ted Striker: Surely you can't be serious.
Rumack: I am serious... and don't call me Shirley.
From the punderfully joke-filled film - Airplane.)

.° ⚠ °.

Boris: You busy-bodies have busied your last body.
- Rocky and Bullwinkle Show

.° ⚠ °.

Bullwinkle: I'd like to apply for a job as an usher?
Boris: What experience have you had?
Bullwinkle: I've been in the dark for most of my life.
- Rocky and Bullwinkle Show

"Beyond the Alps lies more Alps. And The Lord Alps those that Alps themselves." - Groucho Marx

"I intend to live forever, or die trying."
- Groucho Marx

"One morning I shot an elephant in my pajamas. How he got into my pajamas I'll never know."
- Groucho Marx

"Marriage is a wonderful institution, but who wants to live in an institution." - Groucho Marx

"Blessed are the cracked, for they shall let in the light." - Groucho Marx

.° � °.

"Time wounds all heels." - Groucho Marx

.° � °.

"I thought my razor was sharp until I heard his speech." - Groucho Marx

.° � °.

"I like a woman with a head on her shoulders. I hate necks." Steve Martin

.° � °.

"No man goes before his time - unless the boss leaves early." Groucho Marx

.° � °.

"I went to a restaurant that serves 'breakfast at any time' and ordered French Toast during the Renaissance." - Steven Wright

.° � °.

"You can leave in a huff. Or you can leave in a minute and a huff." Groucho Marx

. ° ⊗ ° .

"Die, my dear? That'll be the last thing I do."
- Groucho Marx

. ° ⊗ ° .

"By the time a man is old enough to watch his step, he's too old to go anywhere." - Billy Crystal

. ° ⊗ ° .

"You go Uruguay, and I'll go mine." Groucho Marx

. ° ⊗ ° .

"Oh, why can't we break away from all this, just you and I, and lodge with my fleas in the hills? I mean flee to my lodge in the hills." - Groucho Marx

. ° ⊗ ° .

"The problem with life is, by the time you can read a woman like a book, your library card has expired."
- Milton Berle

. ° ⊗ ° .

"Go, and never darken my towels again."
- Groucho Marx

"It's hard to get ivory in Africa, but in Alabama the Tuscaloosa." - Groucho Marx

"Room service? Bring up a larger room."
- Groucho Marx

"Heifer cow is better than none." - Groucho Marx

"Ice water? Get some onions; that'll make your eyes water." - Groucho Marx

"Show me where Stalin is buried and I'll show you a Communist plot." Edgar Bergan

"I have mood poisoning. Must be something I hate."
— Marilyn Manson

.° ☣ °.

I resemble that remark" - Chico Marx

.° ☣ °.

"I've got a mind to join a club and beat you over the head with it." - Groucho Marx

.° ☣ °.

"What do I look like, an inferior decorator?"
- Archie Bunker (All in the Family TV Show)

.° ☣ °.

"Listen to the blabbing brook" - Norm Crosby

.° ☣ °.

"And he (Mike Tyson) will have only channel Vision."
- Frank Bruno

.° ☣ °.

"It's beyond my apprehension."
- Danny Ozark

"I'd rather have a bottle in front of me than a frontal lobotomy." - Dorothy Parker

. ° ❀ ° .

He hated being thought of as one of those people that wore stupid ornamental armor. It was gilt by association." — Terry Pratchett, Night Watch

. ° ❀ ° .

"What does Karl Marx put on his pasta? Communist Manipesto!" — Steven Colbert

. ° ❀ ° .

From what I've experienced of vampires, you mostly suck. - — Cassandra Clare (City of Lost Souls)

. ° ❀ ° .

"I was pure as the driven snow, then I drifted."
- Mae West

. ° ❀ ° .

"If you are not fired with enthusiasm, you will be fired with enthusiasm."
- Vince Lombardi.

"Did you hear about the Chinese- German restaurant? The food is great, but an hour later, you're hungry for power." - Dick Cavett

★ ★ ★ - ` ❀ ´ - ★ ★ ★

# Daffynitions
## New Definitions for Old Words

A "daffynition" is a pun involving the redefining of an existing word based on its sound being similar to another word or group of words. It can also simply be a humorous or clever definition of a given word, such as, *hangover: the wrath of grapes.*

This pun form was popularized in 1972 by panelists on the BBC Radio 4 quiz show *I'm Sorry I haven't a Clue.* The show ran continuously until 28 December 2020.

Abbreviate: a soft cheese we ate yesterday

Alimony: the high cost of leaving

Alps: give assistance to, as in "every little bit alps."

Antelope: how your mother's sister got married

Aperitif: Two incisors

Appeal: watch out for this after eating a banana

Arch rivals: Competing podiatrists

Avoidable: what a toreador tries to do

Bacteria: rear entrance to a school lunchroom

Brouhaha: amusing tea

Brussels sprouts: young Belgian children

Buccaneer: what the pirate paid for corn

Cannibal: someone who goes to a restaurant and orders the waiter

Chef: a cook with a big hat and a head to fill it

Christmas: a holiday when we sit in front of a dead tree and eat candy from our socks

Dandelion: a fashionably dressed king of the jungle

Debate: what lures de fishes

Decadent: having ten teeth

Departmental: of a mind to quit

Doughnut: the original hole food

Egoist: somebody who is usually me-deep in conversation

Extent: previously a canvas home

Flabbergasted: astounded by how much weight you've gained

Flashlight: a tube for holding dead batteries

Fortune teller: a bank employee who deals only with large accounts

Furlong: shaggy

Gentleman: a man who can play the bagpipes but doesn't

Gladiator: an unrepentant cannibal

Heirloom: a dead giveaway

Hermit: a lady's baseball glove

Heroes: what a guy in boat does

Holstein: an entire beer mug

Hunch: a gut feeling you get during lunch

Hundred: fear of Attila and his hordes

Hypochondriac: a person who won't leave well enough alone

Ignorant: to disregard a tiny insect

Information: how geese fly

Irony: the opposite of wrinkly

Jury: a group chosen to decide who has the better lawyer

Khakis: what you need to start a car in Boston

Kindred: fear of family gatherings

Labor Pain: Discomfort from a work injury

Liability: A talent for hiding the truth

Lobster: a softball pitcher

Locus: a quiet curse

Lymph: To walk with a lisp

Manicurist: a doctor who treats diseases of men

Mendacity: urban renewal

Mosquito: an insect that makes flies seem tolerable

Moray:
When an eel bites your thigh,
And it stings like you'll die,
That's a moray!

Nitrate: The cost of a cheap motel

Octopus: an eight-sided cat

Optimist: a person who smells smokes and gets out the marshmallows

Out of bounds: what happens to an exhausted kangaroo

Pasteurize: in the distance (to see the horizon, look past your eyes)

Pen Pal: pig's correspondent

Porcupine: a craving for bacon

Private call: how low-ranking soldiers contact home

Protein: in favor of youth

Redundant: A politician in a hot air balloon

Reintarnation: coming back to life as a hillbilly

Ricochet: an Irish bouncer

Roughage: approximately how old you are

Second in Command: A short time as a leader

Sherbet: a wager you're certain to win dessert

Shin: what you use to locate furniture in the dark

Shotgun wedding: a case of wife or death

Ski match: a slalom occasion

Stiff competition: competing funeral homes

Toothache: a pain that drives you to extraction

Truth: something that doesn't lie in the open

Vigilante: an observant aunt

Volunteer: takes on work for no sense (cents)

Waffle Iron: an indecisive golf club

Will: a dead giveaway

Zebra: the largest size of female support garment

# It's a Job

## They Lost Their Jobs

When the hotel porter lost his job, he was shown the door.

The farmer was put out to pasture.

The banker was fired because he lost interest in his work.

The baseball player was debased.

The innkeeper was dislodged.

The cowboy was deranged.

The electrician was delighted.

The engineer was ruled out.

The gambler was discarded.

The fisherman was debated.

The musician was decomposed.

The clothing designers and priests were defrocked.

Cashiers and moonshiners were distilled.

Pig farmers were disgruntled.

Truckers are never fired; they just retire.

The skeptic wasn't fired, but his future was uncertain.

The watchmaker wasn't fired, he was just given time to wind down.

The librarian wasn't fired, he just got shelved.

## They Never Die

Old accountants never die, they just lose their balance.

Old judges never die, they just cease to try.

Old chauffeurs never die, they just lose their drive.

Old doctors never die, they just lose their patience.

Old lawyers never die, they just lose their appeal.

Old beekeepers never die, they just buzz off.

Old wrestlers never die, they just lose their grip.

Old painters never die, the just get brushed off.

Old steel makers never die, they just lose their temper.

Old statisticians never die, they just average out.

Old basketball players never die, they just continue dribbling.

Old skiers never die, they just go downhill.

Old sewage workers never die, they just waste away.

Old professors never die, they just lose control of their pupils.

Old pilots never die, they just go onto a higher plane.

Old mathematicians never die, they just pass their prime.

Old florists never die, they just make alternative arrangements.

Old informers never die, they're just put out to grass.

Old cartoonists never die, they just go into suspended animation.

Old bakers never die, they just stop making any dough.

Old limbo dancers never die, they just go under.

Old deans never die; they just lose their faculties.

Old bankers never die, they just want to be a loan.

Old baseball players never die, they just go batty.

Old astronauts never die, they just go to another world.

Old planters never die, they just go to seed.

Old grammarians never die, they just fall into a comma.

Old owls never die, they just don't give a hoot.

# Other Employment Jokes

The surprised gardener had a root awakening

Sign outside an exterminator's office: "We make mouse calls."

A glassblower inhaled and got a pane in his stomach.

The orchestra leader kept throwing tempo tantrums.

Why was the coroner thinking of retiring? He had a dying practice.

What does one surgeon say when taking over for another?
*May I cut in.*

When the old wrestler quit, he handed in his too weak notice.

My job picking vegetables comes with a good celery.

Cleaning mirrors is one job I can see myself doing.

Why did the nuclear plant operator get fired?
*He had a meltdown.*

What's a great job for a spider?
*Web development.*

How did the lawyer learn his job?
*Through trials and error.*

I just got a job at the salt and pepper factory.
It's seasonal.

I had been working at the herb factory, but got fired for wasting thyme.

Why do writers get so cold?
*They're surrounded by drafts.*

I needed money so I got a job as a volunteer. That made no cents (sense).

# Tom Swifties

**"These are Swifties," Tom said rapidly.**

Tom Swift is the main character of a series of American juvenile adventure and science fiction novels first published in the early 1900s. The series was created by Edward Stratemeyer, the same publisher who created The Hardy Boys and Nancy Drew.

The books were written in a style which made use of a distinct phrasing. A Tom Swifty is a one-line joke, based on the writing style used in the original books that turns verbs and adverbs into punchlines.

.° ⚠ °.

"All I care about is getting some air blowing in this room," said Tom fanatically.

.° ⚠ °.

"And that's the mausoleum," Tom said gravely.

.° ⚠ °.

"Between you and me, I just joined the army," Tom said privately.

"Don't fire that gun," Tom shot out.

.° ⚠ °.

"Don't touch my turtle," Tom snapped

.° ⚠ °.

"Elvis has left the building," Tom said expressly.

.° ⚠ °.

"Get that dog out of here," Tom barked.

.° ⚠ °.

"He abandoned me on this cliff," Tom alleged.

.° ⚠ °.

"It's time for me to give you your gift," Tom said presently.

.° ⚠ °.

"It seems like this tooth extraction is taking forever," Tom said with infinite wisdom.

"I have to keep the fire alight," Tom bellowed.

.° ☣ °.

"Here's to hot buttered bread!" Tom toasted.

.° ☣ °.

"I don't know how to start an old Model-T." Tom was cranky.

.° ☣ °.

"I can eat 144 raw hot dogs," Tom was gross.

.° ☣ °.

"I can't drown in this African river." Tom was deep in denial.

.° ☣ °.

"This garbage is making me fat. We should throw it out," Tom said wastefully

.° ☣ °.

"I can't write with this pencil," Tom said bluntly

.° ☣ °.

"I cut off the bottom of my jeans, so they'll stay clean," Tom said hygienically.

.° ⚕ °.

"I don't really like my friend the ugly hippopotamus!" said Tom Hippocritically.

.° ⚕ °.

"I don't care if my deck contains only spades, diamonds, and clubs," Tom was heartless.

.° ⚕ °.

"Some Martian stole all my aces, "Tom wasn't playing with a full deck.

.° ⚕ °.

"I know I can get a table by the window," Tom said without reservations.

.° ⚕ °.

"I keep asking you not to ride that horse," Tom nagged.

.° ⚕ °.

"I know what herb goes best in this turkey casserole," Tom said sagely.

.° ☣ °.

"I don't care if my hands hurt, "Tom said callously.

.° ☣ °.

"I like modern paintings," Tom said abstractedly

.° ☣ °.

"I have a split personality," Tom was frank.

.° ☣ °.

"I have to sing a run of eighth notes," Tom quavered.

.° ☣ °.

"This is where I keep my arrows," Tom quivered.

.° ☣ °.

"despite your warnings, I removed all the feathers from this chicken," Tom was plucky.

.° ☣ °.

"I stole your candy bar," Tom snickered

. ° ☣ ° .

"I think I'll have my afternoon snack with the livestock," Tom stroked his goatee.

. ° ☣ ° .

"I think this line needs more emphasis," Tom said boldly.

. ° ☣ ° .

"Let's milk the cow," Tom uttered.

. ° ☣ ° .

"Let's pet this mixed-breed dog," Tom muttered.

. ° ☣ ° .

"Look! I'm a butterfly." Tom fluttered.

. ° ☣ ° .

"I threw away my extra tire." Tom flatly despaired.

. ° ☣ ° .

"I won't share my seafood restaurant with anyone," said Tom selfishly.

"I'll change your grade on this paper," Tom remarked.

"I'll have a hot dog with everything on it," Tom said with relish.

"I'm off to see my people in Scotland," Tom said clandestinely.

"I'm devoted to the ratio of the circumference to the diameter," said Tom Piously.

"I'm losing my hair," Tom bawled.

"I'm no good at darts," Tom threw out aimlessly.

"My pet vampire is taller than he was yesterday," Tom said gruesomely.

. ° ☣ °.

"I don't mind waiting to see the doctor," Tom said patiently.

. ° ☣ °.

"I've always been afraid of sheep," Tom bleated

. ° ☣ °.

"I've finally seen a mushroom cloud!" Tom was radiant.

. ° ☣ °.

"I probably shouldn't have fed the crocodile," Tom said offhandedly.

. ° ☣ °.

"Is that uranium?" Marie asked curiously.

. ° ☣ °.

"Let's get out of this snake pit," Tom rattled on.

"Let's go dig up some old friends." Tom said gravely.

"Let's transfer this money to another German bank account," Tom remarked with interest.

"My candle has finally gone out," Tom was delighted.

"Not shellfish again!" Tom was crabby.

"Now I can do some painting," Tom said easily.

"Once in a while I don't lose," Tom said winsomely.

"Someday I'm going to be the head of the CIA," said Tom aspiringly.

*.° ☣ °.*

"That was a frightening fairy tale," Tom was grim.

*.° ☣ °.*

"The exit is right there," Tom pointed out.

*.° ☣ °.*

"This game bird is foul," Tom groused.

*.° ☣ °.*

"The average frequency of my voice is 160Hz," said Tom in measured tones.

*.° ☣ °.*

"The size of these cobs is a-maize-ing," was Tom's corny joke.

*.° ☣ °.*

"The wind is really picking up," Tom blustered.

*.° ☣ °.*

"There goes my hat," said Tom off the top of his head.

.° ⚠ °.

"This champagne has lost its bubbles," Tom whined.

.° ⚠ °.

"This is a mutiny!" shouted Tom bountifully.

.° ⚠ °.

"We discussed the afterlife." It was a spirited discussion.

.° ⚠ °.

"I guess the ghosts have all left," Tom was dispirited.

.° ⚠ °.

"We just struck oil," Tom gushed.

.° ⚠ °.

"Yes, I'd prefer a harder mattress," Tom affirmed.

.° ⚠ °.

"You have been found guilty," said the judge with conviction.

"You cannot set that thermostat at 102 degrees Fahrenheit." The argument was getting heated.

"You have the right to remain silent," said Tom arrestingly.

"You should consult an investment broker," was Tom's stock answer.

"You turned on the circuit breaker?!" Tom was shocked.

"Your fly is undone." Was Tom's zippy rejoinder.

"Your honor, I think you're crazy," said Tom judgmentally.

# It's a Mad, Mad, Mad, Mad Magazine

Nothing says brilliant punning and satire quite like MAD Magazine.

Some of the punning brilliance of the writers of Mad appeared in their TV and movie spoofs and song parodies.

What Mad Magazine fan will ever forget the classic 1963 parody East Side Story, a brilliant spoof on the Broadway hit West Side Story. Gems from this musical satire included "When You're a Red" ("When You're a Jet") and "I Feel Vicious" ("I Feel Pretty").

Here are a few more of their musical parodies:
"Stokely and Tess" (A Mad Modern Version of "Porgy and Bess")

"On a Clear Day You Can See a Funny Girl Singing "Hello Dolly" Forever (A Mad combination of the Barbra Streisand musicals "On a Clear day You Can See Forever", "Hello Dolly" and "Funny Girl")

"Porn in the USA" (Born in the USA)

What Mad did for (or against) popular songs, it also did for movies and television.

Here are some original titles followed by their Mad Magazine spoof title. (I wish I could include more of these, but I'm already getting a little carried away with my homage to the timeless humor that poked fun at society and allowed us to laugh at ourselves.

## Television Title Spoofs

The Rifleman / The Rifle, Man (1960)

Naked City / Naked Town (1961)

Bonanza / Bananaz (1962)

Dr. Kildare / Dr. Kiljoy (1962)

The Fugitive / The Phewgitive (1964)

The Man from U.N.C.L.E. / The Man from A.U.N.T.I.E. (1964)

Peyton Place / Passion Place (1965)

Lost in Space / Loused Up in Space (1966)

I Spy / Why Spy? (1967)

Mission: Impossible / Mission: Ridiculous (1968)

The Flying Nun / The Flying Nut (1968)

The Mod Squad / The Odd Squad (1969)

The Doris Day Show / The Doris Daze Show (1971)

Hawaii Five-0 / How-Are-Ya-Five-0 (1971)

The F.B.I. / The F.I.B. (1971)

The Partridge Family / The Putrid Family (1972)

Columbo / Clodumbo (1973)

Kung Fu / Kung Fool (1974)

Kojak / Kojerk (1975)

Happy Days / Crappy Days (1976)

The Bionic Woman / The Moronic Woman (1977)

One Day at a Time / One Dame at a Time (1977)

The Jeffersons / The Jazzyslums (1977)

Fantasy Island / Fantasy Buy Land (1978)

Quincy, M.E. / Queezy, M.E. (1981)

Too Close for Comfort / To Gross for Comfort (1981)

M.A.S.H. / M.U.S.H. (1982)

The A-Team / The A-sinine Team (1983)

Cheers / Beers (1984)

Dynasty / Die Nasty (1985)

Wheel of Fortune / We'll Make a Fortune (1986)

Who's the Boss / Boobs the Boss (1986)

L.A. Law / L.A. Lewd (1987)

The Wonder Years / The Blunder Years (1989)

Home Improvement / Gnome Improvement (1992)

Seinfeld / Swinefilled (1994)

NYPD Blues / NYPD Boobs (1994)

Friends / Fiends (1995)

The Nanny / The Ninny (1996)

The Sopranos / The Supremos (2000)

The Practice / The Malpractice (2000)

Boston Public / Boston Pubic (2002)

Law and Order: Criminal Intent / Lewd & Disorder: Criminal Malcontent (2005)

Pawn Stars / Yawn Stars (2011)

Storage Wars / Storage Boors (2013)

Shark Tank / Snark Tank (2014)

# Movie Spoofs

King Kong / Ping Pong (1953)

Hah! Noon! (1954)

From Here to Eternity / From Eternity to Here (1954)

The Seven Year Itch / The Seven Itchy Years (1955)

The Man in the Gray Flannel Suit / The Man in the Soot-Gray Flannel (1956)

Moby Dick / Morbid Dick (1956)

The Guns of Navarone / The Guns of Minestrone (1962)

The Birds / For the Birds (1963)

The Sandpiper / The Sinpiper (1966)

The Spy Who Came in From the Cold / The Spy Who Came in For the Gold (1966)

The Sound of Music / The Sound of Money (1967)

The Professionals / The Amateurs (1967)

Up the Down Staircase / In the Out Exit (1968)

The Graduate / The Post-Graduate (1968)

Guess Who's Coming to Dinner / Guess Who's Throwing-Up Dinner (1968)

Goodbye Columbus / Hoo-Boy, Columbus (1969)

The Godfather / The Oddfather (1972)

Rocky / Rockhead (1977)

Moonraker / Moneyraker (1980)

Kramer vs. Kramer / Crymore vs. Crymore (1980)

Trading Places / Trading Races (1984)

Yentl / Mentl (1984)

All the Right Moves / All the Right Movements (1985)

Peggy Sue Got Married / Peggy Got Stewed and Married (1987)

Pretty Woman / Slutty Woman (1991)

Presumed Innocent / Presumed Impotent (1991)

The Green Mile / The Yellow Mile (2000)

# That's Punny

Why was the accountant fired from his job at the circus?
*He was caught juggling the books.*

I once spent 24 hours trying to calculate the time it takes for the earth to spin on its axis.
Then I decided to call it a day.

Have you heard about the insomniac dyslexic agnostic who stayed up all night wondering if there really was a dog.

I've heard a few puns about unemployed people but none of them worked.

A man walked into a chimney store and asked "How much for this one?" The salesman replied "It's on the house."

One of these new shoes isn't right.

.° ☣ °.

Two antennas got married. The ceremony wasn't anything special, but the reception was excellent.

.° ☣ °.

What do you get when you mix alcohol and a Harper Lee Classic. Tequila Mockingbird.

.° ☣ °.

A new restaurant opened in town. It's called Karma. There's no menu, you just get what you deserve.

.° ☣ °.

To the guy who invented zero, thanks for nothing.

.° ☣ °.

My grandpa has the heart of the lion and a lifetime ban from the zoo.

.° ☣ °.

I could get you a broken puppet; no strings attached.

I don't like sitting next to Fred the pig; he's such a boar.

.° ⬡ °.

When it comes to pieces of classical music, I like to think outside the Bachs.

.° ⬡ °.

Once you see one shopping center, you've a mall.

.° ⬡ °.

At first, I didn't want the transplant, then I had a change of heart.

.° ⬡ °.

I used to be afraid of hurdles, but I got over it.

.° ⬡ °.

I was going to go on a diet, but I have too much on my plate right now.

.° ⬡ °.

I wondered why the baseball was getting bigger; then it hit me.

·° ☣ °·

Women who wear only $200 perfume have no common scents.

·° ☣ °·

I went to a corn sale at the general store, and was amaized that all they had was colonels.

·° ☣ °·

Some said, no matter to what heights George W. rose in politics, he remained in the Bush leagues.

·° ☣ °·

There are three kinds of people; those who can count and those who can't.

·° ☣ °·

I just couldn't make the costume for the ballerina. It was too-too difficult.

·° ☣ °·

Does the name Pavlov ring a bell?

.° ☣ °.

I didn't go to his funeral. It started at 8AM and I'm not a mourning person.

.° ☣ °.

Unfortunately, we didn't get any cookies with our Chinese dinner.

.° ☣ °.

My animal puns are unbearable and unkoalafied disasters.

.° ☣ °.

Don't drink with spirits if you can't handle the booze (boos).

.° ☣ °.

The man who drove his expensive car into a tree discovered the Mercedes bends.

.° ☣ °.

The inventor of the door knocker won the no-bell prize.

.° ⚠ °.

Show me a piano that fell down a deep hole in the ground and I'll show you A-flat minor.

.° ⚠ °.

I couldn't figure out how to fasten my seatbelt, then it clicked.

.° ⚠ °.

The past, present, and future walked into a bar. It was tense.

.° ⚠ °.

When life gives you melons, you're probably dyslexic.

.° ⚠ °.

One bird can't make a pun. But toucan.

.° ⚠ °.

You can push the envelope all you want; it'll still be stationary.

.° ⚠ °.

The only way I know of to make holy water is just boil the Hell out of it.

.° ☣ °.

Dystopian novels are so 1984.

.° ☣ °.

Why is John Milton a terrible guest at game night? When he's around there's always a "pair of dice lost."

.° ☣ °.

Jane, how do you feel about Charlotte Bronte? She's a breath of fresh Eyre.

.° ☣ °.

How did Voltaire like his apples? Candied (Candide)

.° ☣ °.

Dieting is the triumph of mind over platter.

.° ☣ °.

Hundreds of hares have escaped the zoo. Police are combing the area.

. ° ☣ ° .

Everyone thinks my runny nose is funny, but it's snot.

. ° ☣ ° .

Did you hear about the lumberjack who couldn't hack it. They finally gave him the axe.

. ° ☣ ° .

What do you call a cow who eats the grass in your backyard? A lawn-mooer.

. ° ☣ ° .

I'd like to give a shout 'out' to the people wondering what the opposite of 'in' is."

. ° ☣ ° .

Inspecting mirrors is a job I could really see myself doing.

. ° ☣ ° .

A bipartisan bill legalizing medical marijuana for use in alleviating symptoms of arthritis would be joint support for joint support for joint support!

To whoever stole my Microsoft Office. I will find you! You have my word.

.° ☣ °.

The man who survived mustard gas and pepper spray is now a seasoned veteran.

.° ☣ °.

When she told me I was average, I knew it was just mean.

.° ☣ °.

Response to a tech support request: "To better assist you, our live phone support and chat options will be temporarily unavailable.." (I wonder if they get the irony of this.)

.° ☣ °.

Who actually discovered fire is a subject that's been hotly debated.

.° ☣ °.

German sausage jokes are the wurst.

.° ☣ °.

That vaccination didn't hurt at all. It was a jab well done.

.° ⚕ °.

I used to think I was indecisive, but now I'm not so sure.

.° ⚕ °.

I can't be neutral about electrons, they're so negative.

.° ⚕ °.

If you think puns are bad; poetry is verse.

.° ⚕ °.

The baker refused to give me his bread recipe; he said it was on a knead to know basis.

.° ⚕ °.

I tried to catch her eye, but it rolled off the table.

.° ⚕ °.

Three conspiracy theorists walk into a bar. You can't tell me that's just a coincidence.

.° ⚕ °.

Never date a cross-eyed person. They're always seeing someone on the side.

"A guy walks into a bar and sees 3 pieces of meat hanging from the ceiling. He asks the bartender, 'What's this about?' The bartender replies, 'Well, if you can jump up and slap the meat, you get free drinks for the rest of the night. If you miss, you pay for everyone's drinks for the next hour. You wanna do it?' The guy replies, 'Nah, the steaks are too high.'"

Mittens just jumped into the china cupboard and we're about to have a cat-astrophe.

What do you call a small rodent who won't tell you his name? Anony-mouse.

What do you call a socially conscious Chinese frying pan? A woke wok.

After the pot luck dinner, tryouts will begin for the Nativity play. Everyone will have a chance to eat, drink, and be Mary.

.° ⚛ °.

The ambassador decided not to get vaccinated. He already had diplomatic immunity.

.° ⚛ °.

What did the witch use to make sure her incantations were correct? A spell-checker.

.° ⚛ °.

Doctor: Have your eyes been checked recently?
Patient: No, they've always been blue.

.° ⚛ °.

That pun of a gun was a real pistol.

.° ⚛ °.

That book about Persian humor left me cold. It was farcical.

.° ⚛ °.

You know how the army keeps track of ammunition? With a bullet list.

.° ⚕ °.

I just read a book about noble Japanese warriors. Would you like me to samurais it for you?

.° ⚕ °.

What did the police know about the woman who fell from the balcony. She was killed by a pusher.

.° ⚕ °.

What was so great about Orville and Wilbur. They found the Wright way to get high.

.° ⚕ °.

What do you call a street where psychiatrists live? A psycho-path.

.° ⚕ °.

Why was Robinson Crusoe so efficient? He had everything done by Friday.

.° ⚕ °.

What kind of book did the famous car dealer write?
An auto-biography.

.° ⚕ °.

I wasn't looking forward to seeing the podiatrist, but
decided to take it in stride.

.° ⚕ °.

What do botanists do with their notes? Phylum.

.° ⚕ °.

She wrote her history of calligraphy under two pen
names:: Bic and Mont Blanc.

.° ⚕ °.

The man wanted so much money to participate in the
study they called him a human gimme pig.

.° ⚕ °.

I'd never be a history major. There's no future in it.

.° ⚕ °.

I was reading Russian history. It seems Peter and
Catherine were great, but Ivan was terrible.

A mushroom walked into a bar and announced, "Drinks are on me!" The bartender asked, "Why are you buying everybody drinks?" The mushroom replied, "I'm a fun-gi."

How do famous clothing designers dance?
*Chic to chic.*

The athlete wasn't fit enough to win and was too fit to lose; that made him fit to be tied.

What do you call an arrogant prisoner going down stairs? Con-descending.

What did the hot dog seller say to his boss on the last day of work? Frankfurter memories.

The publisher held the poetry contest as a write-off.

.° ⚠ °.

Why did the topless man travel across the country?
He needed to buy a New Jersey.

.° ⚠ °.

I thought bringing my blanket into the club was free,
but it turned out there was a cover charge.

.° ⚠ °.

When the police officer caught the thief stealing a first
edition, he threw the book at him.

.° ⚠ °.

A will is a dead giveaway.

.° ⚠ °.

What's a Grecian urn? Depends on his job.

.° ⚠ °.

What do you call an eye doctor who appears on an
Alaskan island? An optical Aleutian.

.° ✹ °.

What do you call a broken calculator? A weapon of math disruption.

.° ✹ °.

A hole has been found in a wall surrounding the nudist camp. Police are looking into it.

.° ✹ °.

Why was the married woman looking for a boyfriend? To break up the monogamy.

.° ✹ °.

Can I get pregnant using the rhythm method? It's conceivable.

.° ✹ °.

I can't say a was ever an actress, but one time my foot was in a cast.

.° ✹ °.

I can't stop watching shows about Wonder Woman, Super Girl, and Cat Woman. You might even call me a heroin addict.

To Samuel Johnson, writing the dictionary was the defining moment of his life.

. ° ✾ °.

Did you hear about the man who was held at gunpoint in the flower shop? He was a petrified florist.

. ° ✾ °.

What do you call the fear of being asked "who goes there?" Friend-or-Foe-bia.

. ° ✾ °.

What do call the fear of meeting a red-suited fat man in a confined space? SantaClaustrophobia.

. ° ✾ °.

A camping store was holding a January sale and the manager put a young English student in charge of coming up with the slogan. She printed up flyers announcing, "Now is the Winter Offer- Discount Tents."

. ° ✾ °.

It's not like I'm against headache medicine; I can take it Aleve it.

.° ✾ °.

I was trying to connect my GPS with my accelerator, but was getting nowhere fast.

.° ✾ °.

Who are all those people running out of the music store with stringed instruments? Luters, I imagine.

.° ✾ °.

Some days are worse than others. Today, the plumber appeared drained, the electrician was looking for an outlet, the firefighter got the ax, the plasterer was cracked, and the gardener lost all his money in hedge funds.

.° ✾ °.

The inventor of the Wurlitzer left his organs to science.

.° ✾ °.

The man who was hit by a truckload of Kleenex got some soft tissue injuries.

.° ☣ °.

A ladder has been stolen from local hardware store. Steps will be taken.

.° ☣ °.

Impatient dermatologists make rash decisions.

.° ☣ °.

What do you call a man who spent all summer at the beach? A tangent

.° ☣ °.

Drilling for oil is boring.

.° ☣ °.

What did Spartacus say when the lion ate his wife? Nothing, he was gladiator.

.° ☣ °.

Jackhammer operators like to break new ground.

.° ☣ °.

Bellows operators like to break new wind.

The telegraph operator who sent the same message twice was remorseful.

. ° ☣ °.

Why didn't the investor want to sign up for a 401K? He didn't think he could run that far.

. ° ☣ °.

It was such a beautiful wedding; the guests and the cake were in tiers.

. ° ☣ °.

The organ donor was delivered.

. ° ☣ °.

When the electrician met the air hostess, sparks flew.

. ° ☣ °.

When the dentist married the manicurist, they immediately began fighting tooth and nail.

. ° ☣ °.

Why did the elevator operator call the young businessman son? He brought him up, didn't he?

. ° ⚕ ° .

I lost my mood ring and don't know how I feel about that.

. ° ⚕ ° .

I'm going to start collecting highlighters; mark my words.

. ° ⚕ ° .

Don't ask for too large a loan at one time. You don't want to put all your begs in one ask-it.

. ° ⚕ ° .

My fear of moving stairs is escalating.

. ° ⚕ ° .

History is where it's been, but geography is where it's at.

. ° ⚕ ° .

I was addicted to the hockey pokey, but I turned myself around.

A dry cleaner was just arrested for money laundering - a deal is being ironed out.

· ° ⚕ ° ·

I said I'd give a lecture on eternity. Now, I'll never hear the end of it.

· ° ⚕ ° ·

So what if I can't define apocalypse, it's not like it's the end of the world.

· ° ⚕ ° ·

How did the hippie remove the pan of hash brownies from the oven? With a pot holder.

· ° ⚕ ° ·

The lying tailor remained in business by deceit of his pants.

· ° ⚕ ° ·

I thought I was getting a cold, but it was much achoo about nothing.

· ° ⚕ ° ·

I saw these free corpses by the side of the road. It was a dead giveaway.

Dogs can't run x-ray machines, but CAT scan.

★ ⋆ _ , ` ❀ ´ ` _ ⋆ ★ ⋆

## Food Puns

A Penne for Your Thoughts.

I was going to use the jar of tomato sauce, but it was pasta prime.

Why are herbs so expensive?
*Thyme is money.*

The cheeses were so relaxed; they knew everything would Brie alright.

Why did the deli keep running out of sour pickles?
*They were dill-licious.*

What did bread spread say when he arrived during desert?
*Butter late than never.*

What do you call a macaroni noodle that tries to hide in the spaghetti.
*An impasta.*

The Japanese fried fish was so angry, he had a hard time controlling his tempura.

I knew the coffee pot was in a good mood, when I heard it singing, "Oh What a Brewtiful Morning."

I will never make another date with a croissant, they're just too flaky.

.° ⚠ °.

Catnip and lemon balm fell in love the moment they met. It was mint to be.

.° ⚠ °.

Suzie believed she could eat raw fish, sushi did.

.° ⚠ °.

What did the hot dog say to the bun?
*I mustard-mit, I relish you.*

.° ⚠ °.

What did the French bread say to the bun?
*You're my roll model.*

.° ⚠ °.

Why did the chocolate and the cookie decide to get married?
*They had a great relation-chip.*

.° ⚠ °.

Why did Bosc marry Bartlett?
*The made a great pear.*

.° ⬡ °.

This may sound bananas, but I find you appealing.

.° ⬡ °.

Try to eat your vegetables. All I'm saying is 'give peas a chance.'

.° ⬡ °.

Bread puns happen when you yeast expect them.

.° ⬡ °.

What does the cake maker say to his baker at the beginning of each day.
*Batter up!*

.° ⬡ °.

I must have a purpose in life, the mirror reflected.

.° ⬡ °.

If a vegetarian eats vegetables, what does a vegetarian eat?

★ ★ - , ` ⬡ ´ ` - ★ ★

# A Book About...

I was going to write a book about anatomy, but my heart wasn't in it

I was going to write a book about race.
What happened...did someone beat you to it?

I wrote a book about cousins. People found it relate-able.

I wrote a book about our ancestors... but it's ancient history now.

I was partners in a parachute company - then we had a falling out.

I am writing a book about entryways.
How did you get into that?

My friend wrote a joke book about problems with plastering. It really cracked me up.

I am writing a book about crochet.
*What's the hook?*

I wrote a book about macrame.
*How did you tie it together?*

I wrote a book about forest fires.
*How did you get started?*

I wrote a history of light bulbs. It was a bright idea.

I am writing a book about needles.
*What is the point?*

How to make Pasta" by Al Dente
He wrote a book about do-it-yourself teeth
straightening called, "Brace Yourself".

. ° ☣ °.

A doctor wrote a book on do-it-yourself surgery called "Suture Self".

. ° ☣ °.

I was writing a mystery about chimneys, but it went up in smoke.

*✧•˚:*✧•˚:*✧•˚:*✧•˚:*✧•˚:*✧•˚:

# More Puns

Waking up this morning was an eye-opening experience.

......... .° ☣ °. .........

Long fairy tales have a tendency to dragon.

......... .° ☣ °. .........

What do you use to cut a Roman Emperor's hair? *Caesers.*

......... .° ☣ °. .........

When I was young, I was very poor. But after years of hard work, I'm older.

......... .° ☣ °. .........

I made a pun about the wind but it blows.

......... .° ☣ °. .........

Never discuss infinity with a mathematician, they can go on about it forever.

......... .° ☣ °. .........

My wife tried to apply at the post office but they wouldn't letter. They said only mails work here.

.° ⚛ °.

My friend's bakery burned down last night. Now his business is toast.

.° ⚛ °.

What washes up on tiny beaches? Microwaves.

.° ⚛ °.

My ex-wife still misses me. But her aim is starting to improve!

.° ⚛ °.

What's the difference between a hippo and a zippo? One is really heavy and the other is a little lighter!

.° ⚛ °.

I just found out that I'm color blind. The news came completely out of the green!

.° ⚛ °.

Why should you never tell a pun to a kleptomaniac?
They take things …literally.

. ° ☣ °.

The quickest way to make antifreeze? Steal her coat!

. ° ☣ °.

You really shouldn't be intimidated by geometry…
it's easy as pi!

. ° ☣ °.

I thought my guests enjoyed the home movies, but it
turned out I was projecting.

. ° ☣ °.

How do you stop a charging bull?
*Take away its credit cards.*

. ° ☣ °.

I knew I was near the turkey farm when I saw the
gobblestone driveway.

. ° ☣ °.

The does knew they had won the relay race when they passed the buck.

.° ⚕ °.

The most absorbing thing we found on his desk was a blotter.

.° ⚕ °.

The woman who invented the shag carpet made a nice pile.

.° ⚕ °.

Did you hear about the cat who ate the cheese?
*She waited for a mouse with baited breath.*

.° ⚕ °.

Two weevils became con men at the same time. One was a great success. The other was the lesser of two weevils.

.° ⚕ °.

Velcro is such a rip off.

.° ⚕ °.

A dyslexic poet writes inverse.

.° ☣ °.

I was trying to gather a team for the hide and seek tournament, but I couldn't find what I was looking for.

.° ☣ °.

My picture of the field of wheat came out grainy.

.° ☣ °.

A diminutive psychic on the run from the police is a small medium at large.

.° ☣ °.

My vacuum cleaner sucks.

.° ☣ °.

What do you call a snake that is 3.14 feet long?
A pi-thin.

.° ☣ °.

I can never work out how to get to the gym.

Have you ever tried eating a clock? It's time consuming.

Have you ever tried eating a clock? It's time consuming.

What did the volcano say to his wife?
*I lava you.*

What do you call an upstart English teacher?
*A rebel without a clause.*

I owned a taser once. It was stunning.

How frequently do chemists eat at a table?
Periodically.

I bought a pair of shoes from my drug dealer. I don't know what he laced them with, but I've been tripping all day.

.° ☣ °.

I went shopping for cherries and microphones the other day. Bought a bing, bought a boom.

.° ☣ °.

After a concert, I asked ten puns if they liked the sound quality. The feedback was awful; no pun in ten did.

.° ☣ °.

The first session of the procrastination club has been postponed.

.° ☣ °.

I searched the store for camouflage pants, but couldn't find any.

.° ☣ °.

You should have seen the confusion when the stationary store moved.

.° ☣ °.

I did a theatrical performance on puns. It was a play on words

.° ☣ °.

Sleeping comes so naturally to me, I could do it with my eyes closed.

.° ☣ °.

Why did the lion eat the tightrope walker? He wanted a balanced meal!

.° ☣ °.

The chicken coop only had 2 doors. If it had 4 doors it would be a sedan.

.° ☣ °.

I, for one, like Roman numerals.

.° ☣ °.

Had some mushrooms this morning...breakfast of champignons.

.° ☣ °.

Jokes about 90° angles are all right with me.

.° ☣ °.

I drank a soda at a musical performance. It was Fanta at the Opera.

.° ☣ °.

A sign in the window reads *Cured Meats*. Inside, a salami takes his first steps since the accident.

. ° ⚕ ° .

How did the barber shave time off the speed of his marathon run?
*He knew a short cut.*

When does bread go bad?
*When you yeast expect it.*

. ° ⚕ ° .

If you interrupt a person doing a puzzle, you're likely to hear some crosswords.

. ° ⚕ ° .

He was a big fan of whiteboards and found them remarkable.

. ° ⚕ ° .

The other day a clown held the door open for me. I thought it was a nice jester.

. ° ⚕ ° .

I can't believe I got fired from the calendar factory. All I did was take a day off.

.° ⚛ °.

I saw an ad for burial plots, and thought to myself that's the last thing I need.

.° ⚛ °.

I put all my spare cash into an origami business. It folded.

.° ⚛ °.

What did the librarian say when the books were in a mess? We ought to be ashamed of ourshelves!

.° ⚛ °.

I wanted to learn how to drive a stick shift, but I couldn't find a manual.

.° ⚛ °.

How much room should you give fungi to grow? As mushroom as possible.

.° ⚛ °.

My ceiling isn't the best... But it's up there!!!

·°☣°·

6:30 is the best time on a clock… hands down.

·°☣°·

Confucius say, man who runs behind car will get exhausted, but man who runs in front of car will get tired.

·°☣°·

RIP boiling water. You will be mist.

·°☣°·

I work in a paper factory, where my responsibilities are twofold.

·°☣°·

Last week I called someone a watering hole but I meant well.

# More Books From
# Old Town Publishing

Now, That's Interesting: A Collection of Fascinating Facts

1,500 Weird, Wacky and Fascinating Facts

1,500 More Weird, Wacky and Fascinating Facts

Fun and Fascinating Facts About Food

True Stories and Fascinating Facts: 1950s

True Stories and Fascinating Facts: 1960s

True Stories and Fascinating Facts: 1970s

Attention Curious Kids! Random and Interesting Facts

You are a Badass Everyday: A Lot of Motivation in a Little Book

Miss Kitty's Guide to Healthy Living

For Full List
Visit: https://OldTownPublishing.com